Emmie Martins

6 Love Languages For Her

Attract Him! Addict Him! How To Make A Man Love You!

The 25+ Attraction Factor Secrets

How Men Think & What Men Really Want

+ 19 Rules Every Woman Should Know To Get Him

COPYRIGHT

We support copyright of all intellectual property. Copyright protection continues to spark the seed of creativity in content producers, ensures that everyone has their voice heard through the power of words and the captivity of a story. Uniqueness of culture and content has been passed down through generations of writing and is the DNA of every intelligent species on our planet.

This publication is intended to provide helpful and informative material. It is not intended to diagnose, treat, cure, or prevent any health problem or condition, nor is intended to replace the advice of a physician. No action should be taken solely on the contents of this book. Always consult your physician or qualified health-care professional on any matters regarding your health and before adopting any suggestions in this book or drawing inferences from it.

The author and publisher specifically disclaim all responsibility for any liability, loss or risk, personal or otherwise, which is incurred as a consequence, directly or indirectly, from the use or application of any contents of this book.

Any and all product names referenced within this book are the trademark of their respective owners. None of these owners have sponsored, authorized, endorsed, or approved this book.

Always read all information provided by the manufacturers' product labels before using their products. The author and publisher are not responsible for claims made by manufacturers.

Copyright © 2018 InfinitInspiration

ISBN 78-3-7439-9333-4

Disclaimer

This publication is intended to provide helpful and informative material. It is not intended to diagnose, treat, cure, or prevent any health problem or condition, nor is intended to replace the advice of a physician. No action should be taken solely on the contents of this book. Always consult your physician or qualified health-care professional on any matters regarding your health and before adopting any suggestions in this book or drawing inferences from it.

The author and publisher specifically disclaim all responsibility for any liability, loss or risk, personal or otherwise, which is incurred as a consequence, directly or indirectly, from the use or application of any contents of this book.

Any and all product names referenced within this book are the trademark of their respective owners. None of these owners have sponsored, authorized, endorsed, or approved this book.

Always read all information provided by the manufacturers' product labels before using their products. The author and publisher are not responsible for claims made by manufacturers.

About The Author

Emmie Martins is a professional relationships and dating coach & advisor and has been training women from all walks of life about the many aspects of What Men Really Want!

She is a speaker, author, and publisher of more than 13 extremely popular books on the many aspect of what makes men tick in relation to attraction, love & commitment.

Today she lives with her husband, who she attracted and made fall in love with her by using her own proper system called the 6 Love Languages plus a little mystery trick that she also teaches to her students, in the beautiful area of Sausalito near San Francisco.

She regularly teaches online and offline classes about the wonderful world of flirting, dating, romance, love, commitment, relationships & marriage, mystery/magic and love, self help and love, spirituality and love. She teaches women from the perspective of a woman how to get everything a woman desires from a man and even beyond by using some powerful spiritual laws of the universe.

She takes the best and most powerful secrets of all the concepts and schools of psychology, communication, attraction, spirituality and beyond.

She is helping and empowering women of all walks of life getting what they want from a man. Emmie claims that by applying her tested & proven system, any woman no matter what her decent, age, religion, or circumstances might be can be empowered to get from a man what she wants.

Her **6 Love Languages** and her **Pink Love Now Eternal Love Forever!** systems works for every woman no matter at what relationship stage she is and no matter if she is a beginner or an advanced user. Her tested and proven system works for every woman worldwide.

She has accumulated lots of testimonials from her students who all have been achieving great results with her systems and methods.

Table of Contents

Contents

Copyright 2

Disclaimer 4

About The Author 6

Table of Contents 7

Words To The Wise 9

Module 1: The Basics 10

Chapter 1 10

Chapter Two 15

Chapter Three 17

Chapter Four 19

Chapter Five 22

Chapter Six 25

Chapter Seven 27

Chapter Eight 32

Chapter Nine 35

Chapter Ten 38

Module 2: The Secrets or The 6 Love Languages 41

 Chapter Eleven 41

Chapter Twelve 47

Chapter Thirteen 50

Chapter Fourteen 54

Chapter Fivteen 59

Chapter Sixteen... 64

Chapter Seventeen.. 68

Chapter eighteen... 74

Chapter Ninteen.. 81

Acknowledgments.. 86

Words To The Wise

"The attractive man leads with his heart while restraining it with his head"
–John Alanis, The King of Let 'em come to You!

Module 1: The Basics

Chapter 1

Important To Get Started

Is your man losing interest? Or, have you tried to get to him before only to be disappointed by his snappy answer?

If you answered "Yes" to either of these questions, then this book is for you. In this book, I have simplified the process of how to get him and keep him forever, including the 6 love languages that you must absolutely master in order to win his heart and some powerful conversation starters that every woman needs to have in her toolbox in order to attract him, flirt with him, seduce him, talk to him, and eventually to keep him interested forever. Keep these in your toolbox of love and you'll get everything from him you ever want!

I am not going to lie to you - men used to intimidate me.

There seemed to be this notion that every woman should have this innate ability to cultivate this perfect relationship without any kind of training or knowledge - like it should be in the genes.

But, for me when I was in my twenties, I could never get it right being with a man.

Back then, I would bring my boyfriend home with great anticipation, but most of the time, I would end up with a disappointing relationship.

My conversations would come out too dry or too tough or too weird or just lacked the humor that I was striving for and the relationship quickly turned into a boring one with a quick end.

Soon, I came to the belief the only way to enjoy a relationship was to go on a mission and discover how men really work.

I am an avid explorer of love & preparing and experimenting with a variety of different methods, but I checked men off my list because I could not figure out what was making them tick causing the less than stellar results each time.

I almost gave up, but a friend introduced me to a dating expert and I had to change my perspective once again.

Then, about five years ago, I was posed with a great challenge.

One of my friend's extended family was visiting and one of the men in the group was very attracted to me.

Opportunity knocked and I was motivated to once again meet the challenge of flirting and falling in love!

I dove right in and learned as much as I could about the various techniques from my dating advice friend.

I learned about all the methods and techniques he suggested. But, I went one step further and befriended yet another relationship expert just to get double advice and at that point I was super excited and obsessed to make this relationship work.

This stacked knowledge was a goldmine- the second dating advice guy ate, slept and breathed dating and relationship advice and he gave me some key tips that I shared with you in this book.

In the weeks, before I really started dating my new boyfriend, I took what I learned and put it to the test. He loved my presence and communication skills and with each test I made our relationship got better. He did of course not know what I was doing and thought that I was a natural.

As far as my boyfriend was concerned, everything was great between us!

The relationship was perfect and our friends left impressed with what we had between us, satisfied, and, of course, full of love!

From that point on, I realized that the complex process of flirting, dating, falling in love, keeping a man's interest, getting a man, and keeping him could be broken down into simpler terms.

Since then, I have dated many other men. And, I have continued to improve the process so that any factors that could get in the way of a great relationship were removed from my process.

I am often asked by my friends how I am able to create such perfect relationship that I have developed over the years with my husband. And, so I created a formula to make it step by step for anyone to follow.

The real secret to great love and a great relationship is understanding that most of the factors that get in the way of having a perfect relationship come into play before the relationship actually starts because the prep phase is critical.

This is the reason why I break up this system into two parts. Part 1 - The basics. This is the prep phase that is the most important phase in dating because if you do not prepare yourself you can break your fragile relationship very quickly. If you take the prep phase seriously, you can win his love forever.
Of course, there is more to it because winning a man's heart is a very complex process, but it is very important to take the basics that include the prep phase very seriously. If you skip the prep phase, you risk losing a valuable experience. It is that important so make sure to not skip the prep phase!

In part 2 of the system, I break down the entire process of making a relationship work for you up in what I call my 6 Love Language Formula.

The stages are obvious, but it is the secret tips and techniques within each step that create this no-fail-proof formula:

Love Language 1: How Men Think - The Attraction Factor
Love Language 2: How Men Flirt
Love Language 3: How Men Fall In Love
Love Language 4: How Men Get Out Of The Friend Zone
Love Language 5: How Men Show Love & Commit
Love Language 6: How Men Love Forever & Never Lose Interest

In the following parts and its chapters, I will go through each step and process in formulaic detail and teach you the key success factors required for a perfect relationship that lasts forever.

Finally, I will give you some extra conversation starters and communication secrets that you can apply to every phase you are currently in your relationship. Use these secrets religiously and you will soon win his heart forever.

Okay, let's get started!

Chapter Two

Preparation

Keeping a man interested forever and growing a deep & true relationship is a quest that takes a lot of groundwork. We will study all the instructions of the planning process. That way you will actually think of how you can achieve this goal. The first thing you need to be aware of is the mental part that goes into an achievement like this. Introspection is a big part of the whole process.

Keeping a man interested forever and maintaining a healthy relationship is a long process which takes a lifetime learning experience. You need to be as equipped as possible before getting started with this challenging experience.

One of the ideal ways to determine whether you will be qualified to keeping and growing a relationship on a long-term basis is to look at the everyday habits of some people who already experience such a relationship.

You don't need to assimilate their accomplishments immediately, as that could be next to impossible. Though, you need to be equipped to exert as much energy as they do. Emulate their habits, as they are specifically where you want to be. Furthermore, reflect on these questions:

Are you looking for a long term relationship

Are you looking for a relationship that lasts forever

Are you looking for the love of your life

Ideally, you responded positively to these specific questions. Then undoubtedly being able to keep a long-term relationship is achievable. Kudos for committing to that initial step forward toward achieving your goals by continuing to read!

Following are some preparatory guidelines to get you on your way:

-- Keeping him guessing

Keeping a healthy relationship as well as keeping a man interested is a mental task just as it would be a tangible one. Mentally, you need to be honest and positive and optimistic. Keeping him guessing every day can help you focus on achieving your goals.

-- Remaining gorgeous despite the many months or years that you've spent with him

Regardless of how much you equip to your task of keeping your man interested, it's indisputable that remaining gorgeous despite the many months or years that you've spent with him is a must immediately off the bat. That is the reason it makes total sense to practice all the daily skills of remaining gorgeous (eating healthy, applying some beauty tips, working out, etc., working on your communication skills, working on your attraction skills) despite the many months or years that you've spent with him, before you dive into all the nitty gritty of what else you need to make happen to achieve great love.

-- Sharing as many experiences with him as possible.

The most critical oversight that anyone could experience when seeking to keep a man interested and growing a meaningful relationship is failing on this vital step. If you choose to not consciously practice sharing as many experiences with him as possible, it can be difficult. That is how reliant keeping a man interested is on sharing as many experiences with him as possible. If you are curious how to share as many experiences with him as possible, then keep exploring as we will address that here!

Keeping a man interested in you forever takes heaps of work invested over time. Therefore you will see, the advantageous way to be equipped for this achievement is to give yourself an appropriate amount of time for the preparations so you can succeed. Do this, and growing and sustaining a loving relationship would be much easier

CHAPTER THREE

What Does It Take?

In the process of preparing for and learning about how to keep a man interested forever, be aware of the following. You have a life-changing road ahead. If this were effortless, every woman would achieve it. Many individuals who make the decision to keep a man interested mentally and physically end up not actually achieving it.

Keeping a man interested forever requires your mental strength just as much as it requires your physical strength. Obviously, keeping a man interested forever is very physical, and just by keeping a stable and strong mindset you can equip yourself for victory.

Regardless of how far back you could bother to look, you will find that those who are achieving their goal of their relationship maintain one big thing in common: they knew what they were getting into. They appreciated what it would be like, keeping a relationship interesting forever involved, along with all that was needed for them to achieve their goals. When you interpret what it takes to keep your man interested in You forever, there is nothing to stop You!

Sustaining a relationship is not just a fleeting diversion, or like dating a man for a very short time. To be equipped, you would have to be honest, positive and optimistic, along with being very patient and sometimes forgiving failure.

Ask yourself again: Are you looking for a long term relationship? Remember this question thoroughly, because those who have already kept a man's interest forever have one thing in common: all of them are honest. You also need to be honest in order to make your goal a reality.

You have already considered whether or not you are positive and optimistic when you were asked: Are you looking for a relationship that lasts forever previously in this book.

Pat yourself on the back for making it this far, because this means you obviously have not surrendered. It is a big difference between doing something and desiring to do it. That will come up frequently in keeping a man's interest mentally and physically.

You've already taken a huge step in being equipped to maintain a healthy relationship. Many individuals mess up for a logical reason. They just did not interpret what they are getting themselves into. Keeping a man interested is truly something that necessitates you to be completely determined and prepared. By simply looking further ahead and being sure you are honest and positive and optimistic, you would be taking the first step toward training.

Just know, sharing as many experiences with him as possible is necessary.

Whenever your mind tells you that developing a healthy relationship is beyond reach, just recognize that someone who is sharing as many experiences with him as possible will move past the negativity and keep the focus on the victory.

Let's explore what is necessary to prepare to see that our heads are where we need it to be!

Chapter Four

Starting The Quest

While you are in the preparing process of keeping a man interested mentally and physically, you should never forget that this process really is a never-ending learning experience for you.

You could find that achieving this goal is affecting other areas of your life at the same time. Keeping and sustaining a relationship is a major life choice that shapes you in lots of ways.

In fact, sharing a healthy relationship requires a shift in your judgment. The honest quality that is necessary to keep a man interested in you forever can impact your whole lifestyle. In an instant, you can be demonstrating an honest quality in other areas of life. That is the attractiveness of keeping your man's interest that many people don't see.

Whenever you work on the process, you may be putting forth a great deal of energy. Fundamentally, you are competing against yourself. The positive and optimistic quality which is necessary to achieve your goal, more importantly, enhances your overall life. While you keep a man interested you actually rely on your mind for strength. That is specifically what makes keeping a healthy relationship possible.

The fact is that your daily work on making your relationship work helps you throughout your life. This is undeniable when you start the process. Actions such as remaining gorgeous despite the many months or years that you've spent with him, keeping him guessing, along with sharing of many experiences with him as possible all necessitate skills which you could use throughout life. Developing your relationship over time provides many useful skills, before and when you accomplish your goals.

Winning a man's heart in the end is more than just dating a man. It is a lifestyle choice in numerous ways. Any time you look at it this way, you can realize the various advantages in your life. Metaphorically, it requires a special characteristic to achieve the final goal. It makes sense to allow those benefits to change your life all around.

You may recollect when we explored certain questions. We were in an effort to determine if keeping a man's interest forever was an action that makes sense for you to attempt.

These following questions are ultimately lifestyle questions:

Are you looking for a long term relationship?

Are you looking for a relationship that lasts forever?

Are you looking for the love of your life?

These specific questions are all about the sort of life you might realize. Provided you answered "yes" to all of the questions presented above, you were not just saying you had what it requires to keeping a man interested forever, but more importantly you were confirming the life that you lead.

By considering the role those attributes play in your everyday routines, you are comprehending the role that achieving a healthy long-term relationship plays in life. All rewarding activities necessitate a commitment and keeping a man interested in you forever is no different.

If you are dedicated to accomplishing what you start, your goal can be another marvelous thing which you accomplish in your life. Best wishes on starting the quest towards a more gratifying lifestyle!

Chapter Five

Rules

Preparing for keeping and maintaining a healthy relationship requires an individual, to be honest, positive and optimistic and patient. Sometimes these attributes can be pulled out of someone when certain tips are executed. This section will explore those tips that have been designed specifically to advance those precise attributes.

Preparing for your goal takes a little groundwork. Many of these standards will be instilled in your head during this timeframe. Since you will probably be working on this process forever because it is a never-ending learning experience and you should have a bit of time to devote some energy to these rules.

Rule1: Stay Healthy & Workout Daily To Stay Physically Attractive & Fit

Just keep a journal to track your progress. This is especially helpful when you're working out and training your body daily to stay healthy and in shape and physically good looking, as this will keep on track with your body transformation. This is not the only advantage that reflecting this rule can bring. Also feeling more self-confident and priming your body physically would be additional benefits which also bring the most noticeable outcome.

Rule 2: Eat Healthy Food

Also, remember that those who effectively eat healthy food and keep their body hydrated which helps to achieve an impeccable and beautiful skin will typically celebrate milestones whenever they recognize a positive change. Do like them and celebrate milestones. It is amazing how such straightforward rules can be such a vital factor to achieve a larger goal. Make it a ritual to include these tips into your daily schedule. Furthermore, actually make sure to celebrate milestones whenever he recognizes a positive change because doing so helps you stay motivated and optimistic.

Rule 3: Work On Your Charisma & Communication Skills

You need to unfailingly have your focus concentrated on building charisma and communicative skills. That could challenge you to be more focused when you prepare, and this is definitely worth it. It also helps you sustain physical attractiveness for longer periods of time and be able to keep a positive conversation for longer time periods. Just listen to positive self-help advice to keep a positive attitude. This can build courage and help yourself to trust in you, which will subsequently increase stamina and presence.

Keeping a man interested forever is not like dating a man for one night or having a one night stand. Though any individual can try to keep a man interested forever on the mental and physical level, it requires someone who is patient and honest to really accomplish this objective.

When making a vow to completely prepare, it is your obligation to not fail! Do you recollect when you were asked these few questions:

Are you looking for a long term relationship

Are you looking for a relationship that lasts forever

Are you looking for the love of your life

You proved you are honest, positive and optimistic, and patient just by saying "yes" to all of these few questions. Whenever you keep a man interested forever, these attributes will serve you. If you remember these important rules, and you work out and train your body daily to stay healthy and in shape, and by eating healthy food and by keeping your body hydrated which helps to achieve an impeccable and beautiful skin, and by working on your skills of building charisma and communicative skills, then you will be a woman who gets him in no time!

Chapter Six

Getting Ready Effortlessly

Though there may be plenty of publications available related to keeping a man interested forever, there is one particular message they all reveal: the planning period is absolutely essential. A standard amount of time to keep a man interested in you mentally and physically is on average a never ending learning process. Preparing for such a long experience grants you the necessary strength to achieve your goal.

You are now completely ready to jump into the task at hand. But, first we'll review a few beneficial habits. That way you're as equipped as possible when you get started with the actual process of keeping a man interested forever. The three steps that you should do to get ready to achieve your goal are:

1. remain gorgeous despite the many months or years that you've spent with him

2. keep him guessing and share as many experiences with him as possible

Stack these skills on top of each other and together they make a solid core for your preparations.

As I said before preparing is absolutely essential, and can't be overemphasized. That allows you to totally prepare. Furthermore, it grants you all of the beneficial habits necessary to achieve your goal. You may find that working out and training your body daily to stay healthy and in shape and physically looking amazing, eating healthy food and keeping your body hydrated which helps to achieve an impeccable and beautiful skin, and building charisma and communicative skills will all ensure that you exert your greatest effort possible.

Any time you disregard these actions, you can forego feeling better about yourself and your body, feeling more self-confident, and priming your body physically. Those results all stem from the all important planning period.

With the proper groundwork and prep, you can certainly achieve the skills of sustaining physical attractiveness and being able to endure a positive conversation with a man for longer periods of time, increasing stamina and presence along with increasing your flirt skills and spontaneity. Each one of those is absolutely essential to plan for and apply in order to achieve a long lasting and well functioning relationship. The greatest part of this is, if you were to put a bit of energy into getting ready, then this could actually be quite effortless for you. So keep from darting over the preparation steps. And finally, make sure that you are totally ready.

Oftentimes, when studying people who productively are able to keep a man's interest forever, it can be easy to feel that they maintain phenomenal strength or know some special secret or trick which qualifies them to achieve deep love.

However, there is no secret. Keeping a man interested forever just needs someone who is honest, positive, optimistic and patient. By simply making the time to be certain that your efforts are effectively working, you will be qualified to achieve the same deep love as those who seem to know these secrets.

In summary, the easiest technique to keeping a man interested forever is to reflect all the steps laid out here. Besides, cutting corners is truly not worth the energy and should be avoided from the beginning.

You need to devote your energy to the preliminary process of the experience as it would make you more successful.

So, make the vow, put in the needed amount of time, and you will achieve your goal in keeping a man interested forever in no time!

Chapter Seven

Hacks To Look Your Best

You may feel that it costs a great deal of money to prepare for your achievement, but in fact you can tap into unlimited resources to do so for free. The key thing you should do when you get down to business is stripping the existing thoughts you may have about what it is like.

Instead, devote your energy to the preparation. Keep in mind, working out and training your body daily to stay healthy and in shape and to keep your good looks is essential and I will show you how to do this on a budget. Good eating habits that include healthy food are essential, too, and keeping your body hydrated which helps to achieve an impeccable and beautiful skin, as well as building charisma and communicative skills are integral steps to get equipped for your goal of keeping a man interested forever. All of these skills can be built up via very economical and sometimes even free resources.

You do not have to go broke to win a man's heart and not having enough money should never be an excuse for you.

Don't throw away lots of money for clothing to impress him because you can look beautiful without artificial and fancy clothing, too.

Investing too much money will not benefit you more in achieving your ultimate goal. So, do not go seeking for shops to spend your savings when you are preparing.

You do not have to spend a lot of money for beauty products, instead learn how to make your own healthy natural beauty products that do cost less, but that are more natural and less harmful to your skin. There are typically free or low-cost alternatives that achieve what you may be attempting to do.

Get free beauty products by participating in Free Beauty Giveaways & Contests. Instead of paying premium prizes you might as well get fancy beauty stuff for free. Search your favorite search engine for these items and you will never have to pay premium prizes for fancy stuff anymore.

Use Coupons:

Always try to think out of the box how could you get something you want for cheaper or free. Use the search engines and marketplaces that offer great daily deals and offers. Use daily deal sites where you can get a cheap prize for a very limited time window.

Here you can find even the best quality beauty products that you love, but that are just too expensive to afford.

What the heck is crowdfunding?

Heck you could even try to fund your project and get money for it via sites like:

kickstarter.com
crowdfunding.com
indiegogo.com

What else could you do to save money?

While you're building charisma and communicative skills, do it with a mentality to save money. Make sure to follow a diet or go through a workout training that costs less money like spending money on fresh fruit and veggies from the farmers market and learning a body training program that you can even perform at home like yoga, for example.

You really do not have to spend money on overly expensive products when there are low-cost alternatives which work just as great. Always choose the natural and cost effective alternative to the high prized stuff because you do not want to pay an exaggerated premium just to get a brand name. Look at the ingredients list and compare to the lower prized alternative product and you will see that most of the times the less expensive prized one features exactly the same ingredients. Often the less expensive stuff provides you with the essentials and does not include unproven and harmful ingredients.

Also, make sure to use coupons and free giveaways if you want to get the fancier stuff.

Here are my favorite coupon sites that I hit weekly to find out the latest beauty coupons, deals & giveaways:

slickdeals.net
fatwallet.com
upromise.com
dubli.com
udemy.com

Only get courses via coupons on udemy which makes the course free. Find these udemy coupons via searches like free coupons udemy and most of the time you get lucky and find courses that are relevant to topics that you are looking for.

I have picked up udemy courses on charisma building, personal development, fashion and communication that regularly cost $500 for free just by doing these searches. Get on their mailing list where they also notify you when coupons are available which usually happens around the holidays.

Don't forget the app market because there you will find an array of apps that deal with couponing and saving money.

Giveaway Sites:

I just love enhancing my beauty and stay updated religiously. If you love to combine the secrets of beauty to attract even more love than you are just like me a beauty & love nut. I am totally into cute and pink beauty products and have joined forces with a supplier who gives me a good deal for my favorite pink love brushes.

To show my love for these and support beauty & love I am regularly holding weekly giveaway until my supplier is out of stock and then I will probably be looking for a new one and still offer these weekly prizes because I love these products so much and like to share my passion by celebrating love & beauty on a weekly basis.

I feel blessed with everything that I have achieved with love and I already told you about my take on celebrating success and results.

I asked you throughout the course to celebrate your results and track them down in your personal journal and celebrate your results.

What other options do you have?

The greatest suggestion is to keep your main focus as the first priority. More specifically, working out and training your body daily to stay healthy and in shape, eating healthy food and keeping your body hydrated, building charisma and communicative skills are areas you may want to focus your spending efforts on. Apply everything you have been learning in this chapter while you are building up your skills. Just focus on your spending habits and get better at identifying the best and most economical buys so that you can satisfy your main priorities.

Later you can stack more on top of it.

While you really review your behavior, it's much easier to recognize when you're squandering money on stuff you don't need.

Working out and training your body daily to stay healthy and eating well does not necessitate a great deal of money.

The objective is to feel better about yourself and your body, and this should be achieved with no spending as it does not need to be pricey. In fact, it naturally costs more to not eating healthy.

For hydration you should always prefer water. Not from the tab, but your favorite source water and not with bubbles but plain. This should not be very expensive and you can also buy in bulk to drop the price even further.

The reason you need to focus on eating healthy food and keeping your body hydrated is so you can boost energy on all levels. Again, this does not necessitate a great deal of spending to achieve. And it costs less money to buy your food at places like the farmer's market instead of the expensive supermarket. Not only is this the way to go if you are on a budget, but in the end the natural food will help you keep the doctor away which in the end is way cheaper than spending on fancy food with weird ingredients and chemicals plus a huge doctor's bill in case your body gets sick from these processed and chemical rich foods.

Building charisma and communicative skills is another thing that you should be really focused on because it's extremely essential for anyone who expects to keep a man interested forever. Though there could be expensive alternatives that seem good, you should learn how to build charisma and communicative skills without having to pay for it.

Just search the internet for terms like:

How to improve my charisma skills
How to improve body language
How to become a better communicator
How to influence others via communication
The law of attraction in communication

and similar phrases and you should be coming up with a work list in not time.

You can get started with some very powerful psychological secrets that will teach you about communication, body language, charisma and other little tricks to get his attention in just 1 Day.

Ultimately, if you stay determined on your objectives, then you should avert wasteful spending to achieve your goal of keeping a man interested forever. There are typically alternatives available that would be minimal in cost. Comprehending the way your feelings influence your spending will guide you to control expenses when you're working towards your goal of keeping a man interested forever.

CHAPTER EIGHT

Step By Step Process

Now that you understand who is inclined to succeed when it comes to keeping a man interested forever, you also understand who will not likely date a man for a short period of time. You understand the attributes that a woman who will achieve her goal has to offer, and now we can start the preparations in even further detail. More specifically, let us talk about exactly the basics of how to keep a man interested forever.

Certainly, the preliminary step is confirming that you are absolutely working out and training your body daily to stay healthy and in shape as this will determine your readiness to keep a man interested forever.

You should think of the details of working out and training your body daily to stay healthy and in shape. Be aware that no women can possibly keep a man interested without taking care of her body and looks because men are very optical oriented. You must be willing to care for your body and health or else you will find your man in the arms of a woman who can.

Be totally aware of the fact that that it is completely impossible to keep a man if you get lazy about these things - that is precisely how vital this step is.

Working out and training your body daily to stay healthy and in shape and physically good looking offers lots of spectacular advantages. For example, it constantly results in you feeling better about yourself and your body.
A different advantage of working out and training your body daily to stay healthy and in shape is it can have you feeling more self-confident.

Furthermore, eating healthy food is necessary to keep a healthy relationship growing. There are obviously numerous results for this. Boosting energy on all levels, though, is considered the most helpful advantage. Without boosting energy on all levels, you can guess that it can be next to impossible to productively keep and maintain a healthy and vital relationship that consists of mental and physical efforts.

The additional results of eating healthy food, as it pertains to keeping a man interested forever, include looking younger with a beautiful body and glowing skin and without having a stressed appearance. In fact, if you're not doing some sort of step into relieving stress, then it may be next to impossible to achieve anything substantial. So, if you opt against keeping your man interested forever, then you still may want to try things that result in relieving stress. Yoga and meditation in combination as well as a healthy sleeping ritual are a secret combination that you might want to give a try if you have not decided on the type of workout you might want to get into.

Once you begin applying your basics that we have been establishing earlier and working out and training your body daily to stay healthy and in shape, you will see that you can not live without this daily routine anymore because it does so much more for you. Just build your workout into your daily framework and remember your averages when you're establishing your timelines.

Do so for the other basic items that you are going to establish a daily routine for and you are set with the basic step by step training.

So make sure that on the last step of the preparatory process, make sure to devote a bit of energy on building charisma and communicative skills. It is easy to neglect steps which are purposefully designed for helping grow your relationship into the right direction. Though, just by focusing your energy upon this precise purpose, you can find that you're able to sustain physical attractiveness for longer periods of time and be able to keep a positive conversation for very long periods of time. Furthermore, building charisma and communicative skills primes you to increase stamina and presence and it helps you with increasing flirt skills and spontaneity as well. All these stages of communication and personality development are important skills that you need to master in order to move on with your relationship.

Ultimately, you'll be equipped to keep a man interested forever just by working out and training your body daily, eating healthy food, and building charisma and communicative skills. Later you can add more to your list, but focus on the basic ones for now.

At that point, you will be able to focus on working out and training your body daily to stay healthy and in shape and physically keep your good looks, along with eating healthy food and keeping your body hydrated which ultimately helps to achieve an impeccable and beautiful skin. Thereafter, you will find that your entire body & mind will help you achieve your goal by working in synchronicity if you are actually applying what you have planned out in the prep phase.

Do your daily ritual religiously and you will be rewarded with an everlasting love!

Chapter Nine

Strategies

Keeping a man interested forever would be a life-changing experience, however, there are some ideas to make your lifestyle a lot more manageable when you are working on your goal. Following are a few tips that can help you.

- Already discussed in the chapters before was the necessity of working out and training your body daily to stay healthy and in shape and physically attractive. It is essential that when you work out and train your body daily, you keep a workout journal to track your progress. This can help keep you on track with your body transformation. That is essential not just when working on your relationship, but in additional areas as well.

- You should understand that eating healthy food and keeping your body hydrated might become hard to make happen on your own. So a good technique to stay motivated and optimistic is to celebrate milestones whenever he recognizes a positive change in you. This will give you additional reasons to keep on track.

- It might seem hard to stay focused on building charisma and communicative skills though this is essential to the ambitions of keeping a man interested forever. It makes sense to listen to positive self-help advice helping you to keep a positive attitude. This can build courage and trust you.
- Here are a few resources that you might consider: My most guarded secret to find free premium courses that normal people pay $500 for every day is to use udemy coupons to get the same course for free. They always run promos and coupons and it is just a matter of investing a little time to find the ones you like and a matching coupon.

While you reflect these effortless suggestions in your preparation for your goal, you will find that you may be gaining many results.

Following are certain results which you will recognize when you see through on your commitment to keeping a man interested forever:

Just remember feeling better about yourself and your body can happen much more intensive as long as you're working out and training your body daily.

- Working out and training your body daily to stay healthy and in shape also allows you to start feeling more self confident and more empowered on all levels.

- Eating healthy food and keeping your body hydrated can result in boosting energy on all levels.

- Eating healthy food and keeping your body hydrated extends lots of results. For example, you can find it easier to look younger with a beautiful body and glowing skin.

- While you strive to building charisma and communicative skills, you may find that you may be increasing stamina and presence.

- Building charisma and communicative skills also will increase your influence and attraction factor.

Keeping a man interested in you mentally and physically grants a great deal of direct results, a handful of which we have already examined like relieving stress, and priming your body physically. All these results occur when you're working out and train your body daily and when you eat healthy food and keep your body hydrated, and when you develop your personality skills like building up charisma and communicative skills. Keeping a man interested in you for a very long time requires carrying out all of these steps and then enjoying the results that follow. Furthermore, following are a few additional tips:

- Don't throw away lots of money for clothing to impress him because you can look beautiful without artificial and fancy clothing, too. Natural is always better than artificial!

- You do not have to spend a lot of money for beauty products, instead learn how to make your own healthy natural beauty products that do cost less and are more natural and less harmful to your skin.

- Make sure to follow a diet or go through a workout training that costs less money like spending money on fresh fruit and veggies from the farmers market and learn a body training program that you can even perform at home like yoga, for example. Yoga in connection with a mental skill like meditation is even better.

Keeping a man interested forever takes a great deal of work. Fortunately, if you use all the guidance offered here that you can take on when you actually get into the action steps, keeping a relationship interesting and a love deep, then you will be more than qualified by the end of the day to keep your man very interested in you.

The suggestions which would be noted here serve a starting point. When reading this information, you'll have a very basic understanding of all that it takes to keep a man interested forever. It is up to you to use the information to your own advantage. So go through the prep phase by making mental notes and by planning out what you have learned in the step by step chapter and the strategy chapter and put it into a daily framework and then actually act upon it. Put your framework into action.

Later once you master the basics described in module 1 of this course, you can stack more items that would influence and shape your love and relationship positively onto your list.

For now, feel free to add your individual reflections and make new recommendations to what is working for you and what you should be changing to make it better as you go through your basic daily ritual. A journal is a great way to keep track of this entire process.

Taking active part in this process is encouraging you be successful.

Chapter Ten

Common Questions

Keeping a man interested forever would be a life-changing experience, however, there are some ideas to make your lifestyle a lot more manageable when you are working on your goal. Following are a few tips that can help you.

- Already discussed in the chapters before was the necessity of working out and training your body daily to stay healthy and in shape and physically attractive. It is essential that when you work out and train your body daily, you keep a workout journal to track your progress. This can help keep you on track with your body transformation. That is essential not just when working on your relationship, but in additional areas as well.

- You should understand that eating healthy food and keeping your body hydrated might become hard to make happen on your own. So a good technique to stay motivated and optimistic is to celebrate milestones whenever he recognizes a positive change in you. This will give you additional reasons to keep on track.

- It might seem hard to stay focused on building charisma and communicative skills though this is essential to the ambitions of keeping a man interested forever. It makes sense to listen to positive self-help advice helping you to keep a positive attitude. This can build courage and trust yourself.
- Here are a few resources that you might consider: My most guarded secret to find free premium courses that normal people pay $500 for every day is to use udemy coupons to get the same course for free. They always run promos and coupons and it is just a matter of investing a little time to find the ones you like and a matching coupon.

While you reflect these effortless suggestions in your preparation for your goal, you will find that you may be gaining many results.

Following are certain results which you will recognize when you see through on your commitment to keeping a man interested forever:

Just remember feeling better about yourself and your body can happen much more intensive as long as you're working out and training your body daily.

- Working out and training your body daily to stay healthy and in shape also allows you to start feeling more self-confident and more empowered on all levels.

- Eating healthy food and keeping your body hydrated can result in boosting energy on all levels.

- Eating healthy food and keeping your body hydrated extends lots of results. For example, you can find it easier to look younger with a beautiful body and glowing skin.

- While you strive to build charisma and communicative skills, you may find that you may be increasing stamina and presence.

- Building charisma and communicative skills also will increase your influence and attraction factor.

Keeping a man interested in you mentally and physically grants a great deal of direct results, a handful of which we have already examined like relieving stress, and priming your body physically. All these results occur when you're working out and train your body daily and when you eat healthy food and keep your body hydrated, and when you develop your personality skills like building up charisma and communicative skills. Keeping a man interested in you for a very long time requires carrying out all of these steps and then enjoying the results that follow. Furthermore, following are a few additional tips:

- Don't throw away lots of money for clothing to impress him because you can look beautiful without artificial and fancy clothing, too. Natural is always better than artificial!

- You do not have to spend a lot of money for beauty products, instead learn how to make your own healthy natural beauty products that do cost less and are more natural and less harmful to your skin.

- Make sure to follow a diet or go through a workout training that costs less money like spending money on fresh fruit and veggies from the farmers market and learn a body training program that you can even perform at home like yoga, for example. Yoga in connection with a mental skill like meditation is even better.

Keeping a man interested forever takes a great deal of work. Fortunately, if you use all the guidance offered here that you can take on when you actually get into the action steps, keeping a relationship interesting and a love deep, then you will be more than qualified by the end of the day to keep your man very interested in you.

The suggestions which would be noted here serve a starting point. When reading this information, you'll have a very basic understanding of all that it takes to keep a man interested forever. It is up to you to use the information to your own advantage. So go through the prep phase by making mental notes and by planning out what you have learned in the step by step chapter and the strategy chapter and put it into a daily framework and then actually act upon it. Put your framework into action.

Later once you master the basics described in module 1 of this course, you can stack more items that would influence and shape your love and relationship positively onto your list.

For now, feel free to add your individual reflections and make new recommendations to what is working for you and what you should be changing to make it better as you go through your basic daily ritual. A journal is a great way to keep track of this entire process.

Taking active part in this process is encouraging you be successful.

Module 2: The Secrets or The 6 Love Languages

Chapter Eleven

How Men Think – Love Language 1

These keys to how men thing and what men desire are not hard to achieve if one knows what to look for. These attraction factors that you need to identify and understand are much easier than many women would think. Women have a complex way of thinking and analyzing whereas men are satisfied with thinking about the simple stuff. Here are 5 few key secrets to getting you started with working on your attraction factor.

The Secrets (Love Language 1)

- Beauty
- He feels good around You
- You forgive him easily.
- Confidence is very sexy.
- Your smile has power

The Bottom Line

The bottom line with comprehending how attraction works in men is simple because it is based on 5 key points that you can easily work on. If you apply some basic beauty rules and communication skills that you discovered in part 1 of this system, you will become very good at this in no time.

Do not make the mistake and overthink this because if you do it might just backfire.
You just have to accept the situation that men are much simpler creatures than women think. Your natural and beautiful smile is important to him so make sure to smile more and you will automatically look great without trying too hard. Be like a friend that he can trust and be easy to be around. Be natural and do not criticize or nag. Forgive easily and certainly make sure not to act as if the world depends on him showing a sign or calling you back. As you get better and better at these skills, his attraction will increase little by little.

The Details

• Attraction

Attraction is without a doubt a necessary part in every relationship no matter at what stage you are, but remember that this notion goes just beyond a simple hip-to-waist ratio.

When he is thinking about you he is asking himself questions like Does she take care of herself? Is she healthy overall? Is she constantly striving to look in a way that will make me feel proud and excited to be with her?

Although you might be aware of the fact that he will never say explicitly, when he is thinking about taking that next step with you.

Just like you he is wondering what your kids might look like. He will also think about the fact of how exactly you will take care of your kids. He will look at how you are taking care of yourself to get a first clue to making that next step and long term commitment.

• Being with you is "easy."

What does this involve? It means no drama and no pressure because a man does not like to sweat the complex stuff.

He just likes hanging out with you in an easy and mentally non-threatening environment.

Think about your own friendships. Why are you comfortable in such an environment? You enjoy being with them because they do not give you a hard time and it is easy being with them. You can reveal your true self and not just an image of you and that is the reason why you love spending time with them. A man has exactly the same concerns and chooses a woman based on these factors.

When he feel this friendship, he wants to be around you more. So, use this knowledge to your benefit!

• You make him feel amazing

Do you love getting compliments? I guess so! If you do so does he so make sure to push his ego buttons on a regular basis. When he always feels amazing in your companion because you give him compliments, he will want to be more often with you.

Why do you think it is that men cheat? Not because you give him enough compliments, but because he does not receive enough. If he committed to you and you stopped doing this for him what do you think will happen?

Men carry fragile egos, which means number one their ego buttons can easily be pushed by any other woman who knows about this secret and number two it does not matter whether a man is committed or not to that other woman who knows how to treat him right.

It is up to you to control the situation. If you push that ego button and tell him how great he is you make him stick around more often or if you really do it well you make him take things up a notch.

• He knows he makes her happy

Do you know that men think like this? It is a man's job to please a woman. Funny for us women but it is true that men at every social level feel an ego boost when they are aware of having made the woman in their life happy and satisfied. It gives them a sense of accomplishment.

So for them it is important to get that kick out of it. Imagine then if you come around always complaining and nagging!

Do you think he will want to commit? No way! He will not feel that he is doing a good job of satisfying you. If he knows beyond for sure because you give him positive feedback that he is capable of making you happy, he will of course stick around you.

• You are different

Dare to be different! Men do not want to marry girls who act just like another girl they already enjoyed. Men that want to commit want a girl that is not easily swayed.

Listen to a man's conversation and that is what they are talking about. I recently overheard a conversation between men and it went like this "She was just … different than any other girl I dated." She's unique, she's different, she's just … I don't know how to say it, but I just know in my gut there is nobody else like her. "

Guess what this man proposed to the lady he was talking about a couple of days later!

Men see the difference and you can take this knowledge to your fullest advantage.

You can even stack a bit mystery on top of your quality of being unique and be as natural as you can and he will totally be yours!

- **She shares feelings easily**

As opposed to women, men aren't as quick to express their feelings. Men are more interested in sharing their feelings than you would believe. You have to listen to him and understand his feelings, too. If you don't you will lose him because he will be wandering off until he finds a girl who he knows will share his feelings with him on a confidential level.

- **She doesn't try to convince him that he needs to**

Relationships do not move to the next level based on one single conversation that you might feel is the most important talk ever.

Guess what? A relationship is a never ending process and experience and you only move to the next level and scale it up a notch because of what happened and because of your aforementioned variables rolled into one.
He trusts you over time and over time, you have become that special woman who has made him feel amazing about himself and he really does not want to lose you.

He does not fall in love with you or decide to commit all of a sudden because you decided to sit him down for an important conversation that ends for him with two options and that is either getting serious or ending the relationship.

Getting him to commit and making him fall in love forever is not about preparing and planning that special night including that one all important conversation because if you act like this you will not get anything out of him.

He is all about the experience and the action part of your relationship and that is exactly what
makes him feel the way you want him to feel for the rest of your love story together.

CHAPTER TWELVE

How Men Flirt – Love Language 2

In order to win a guy's heart, you first need to discover the second love languages because understanding how a man flirts is just another part of cracking the male communication. Flirting is a big part of the whole picture and mastering the second step of this love language system is what you will be discovering below.

Like most women who try to crack the flirting code, you are probably too afraid of making a huge mistake and losing all your worth and credibility in the eyes of that guy.

Powered by my flirting tips, you will never have that problem again.

Here are my 7 secrets to decode a man's flirting ritual. You will get to him if you understand what specifically he is looking for. If you miss just one little detail, you might risk losing him forever so make sure to study these, integrate these into your communications system and track your results.

The Secrets (Love Language 2)

1. Men are looking for signals

If a guy catches your eyes, make it a point to look at his direction because men need little signals.
Repeat a couple of times. He will notice it and then when he is aware of it, give him an ever-so-sly smile that will draw his attention. Just look at him for mere seconds then look somewhere else.

This sign will let him know that you are interested in him.

It is a fun game and especially in a room full of other people.

Do not abuse this because if you do it too often this might make you look a bit creepy in his eyes.

2. He improves his appearance for you

Did you know that men pay attention to how they appear in front of you? They really are and they are very interested in doing it right. They just want to impress females with their appearance.

3. He is trying to hold your look longer than needed

Eye contact is very important in the flirting phase. Eye contact is necessary for every conversation you have with a man, but especially for a man who is flirting and who is interested, he will be trying to prolong the gesture of gazing at you as if to tell you he is intrigued by you. So watch out for these specific gazing looks from him because this is proof enough that he is interested in you and that you appeal to him.

4. He gets physical

When I say physical I mean touching your hair, shoulder, arm, hand, etc. Have you ever heard of the imaginary dust?
He is using this imaginary dust to show affection and he shows it by brushing it away from your clothes. A man will make all kinds of excuses he can find just to get to touch you.

5. He demonstrates subconscious body gestures

Look for the following gestures because these are all signs of showing interest in you. If you get it, you can go from there. The beautiful thing about detecting these signs is that you can kind of control the flow and if you like to get to know that man you can apply what you are learning here. You also have the choice to disconnect and not engage in the flirting ritual at all because you are able to detect these signs now.

So, by now you have a good idea if he is flirting with you. You will now be able to detect if the man is flirting or not. It also shows that men are simpler beings than we women because they are just

going to show it in a very obvious way if they are interested in you. You do not have to do very much on your part except engaging in it or just not paying attention to it.

A woman would act completely different. If you learn to understand and to observe him and his flirting rituals you will soon master this phase and be able to move to love language number 3.

Chapter Thirteen

How Men Fall In Love – Love Language 3

I The truth is you can't make anyone love you, man or woman, but you can create a relationship and you can create an exciting experience that will inspire him and motivate him to love you exactly the way you love him.

Here are the 7 Secret Steps You Need To Know.

The 7 Secrets (Love Language 3)

• Easy Come Easy Go

Remember the film Easy Come, Easy Go? If you do great because remembering this title will give you an aid to remember secret 1 that goes like this. Girl, be as easy and as natural as you can to be around.

Too simple for us women to even consider a fact like this, but easygoing is in the top five list of traits that most men are looking for when they are identifying "the one."

If you are like obnoxiously texting him 77 times a day to discover where he is and what he is about to do, you are not doing a favor to neither of you two. All you are doing is wasting precious time and energy.

• Feed his ego

It may sound sexist and cliche, but it really works for both him and you. You want to be around people who give you nice compliments or make comments about your accomplishments.

Well, so does he! He wants to be around people who make him feel nice, too! You want him to say things to you like that you are beautiful, and likewise he has a desire for such compliments as much as you do.

It is not enough to say the compliment out loud because there is an art to complimenting him appropriately. You need to do it in a congruent way that is natural and you need to do regularly without looking like an obnoxious spy.

Practice the art of giving compliments. Every time your man picks you up, tell him that his new sweater perfectly match his eyes and make him look so handsome. Then reciprocate a compliment for every nice thing he says about you.
It doesn't sound exaggerated, unnatural or fake if it isn't intended to be fake, and feeding his ego like this will make him want to be with you more often and longer. Just don't make it look like a pattern and be as natural about it as you can and he will melt in your hands.

- **Take the initiative once in a while**

As much as he loves the thrill of being the one who is chasing you, he loves to know that you want him, too! So make sure that you do chase him back once in a while. This reciprocity not only feeds his ego and makes him feel good, but it also takes some of the pressure off of his back. Men will not chase women that in their mind they think they can not get them.

If you chase him a little bit here and there, he will know that he will be able to get you and falling in love with you faster than you ever thought possible is what you are trying to achieve her. Don't abuse it, but play with it and empower both of you. This works each time so make use of it.

- **Always smell great**

Did you know that the sense of smell is more important than looks because it triggers much deeper responses in men than looks alone ever can trigger? The smell system in a man's brain (the olfactory system) is strongly connected to the feeling system in the brain (the limbic system).

That is why you get a fuzzy and warm feeling every time you smell your mama's roast in the oven. Smelling triggers these emotions in your man that make him want to be with you. Unlike looks, whenever he smells these things that remind him of you when you are not around him, he will immediately have the trigger happen to him and automatically think of you as an association.

This is a powerful trigger that you can use to make him think about you. It is a real secret because not many people know and use this.

- **Be open**

Once again, men will not drop those three little words that you want to hear all the time. They only express their love until they know without a shadow of a doubt that you are going to say it back to him.

If you are cool and distant and busy with your own life, or if you are guarded and too intimidated to open to him, he will back off each time because you are no longer a sure thing for his ego.

Falling in love is one of the hardest steps for him, but once you make it as easy and as effortless for him, it's nothing but sweetness after that.

Remember if you follow these easy rules you can get everything from him.

- **Need him**

Think back to the primal hunting issue of men. When men have the impression and feeling that they are like the only ones that are capable of providing or helping one special woman, their alpha instinct crops up and they want to be around her to help and protect her more to make sure she is safe. You can be confident and capable and sexy all at the same time, but still ask him to open a hard to open can for you once in a while and he will just love you for it.

- **Whisper in his ear**

There is something about a woman whispering in her man's ear that makes him feel sooooo special. It's almost naughty, but at the same time it is intimate. It is a sizzling combination of something that you want to hide or a secret and a very intimate moment and it works all the time. It proves to him that you are telling him something that you are not telling somebody else, and this secret makes him feel special and when he feels special around you, it leads to a trigger which creates a bonding moment between him and you that you just will not be able to trigger with trying to get his senses with wearing the sexiest dress that you can find in town.

The Bottom Line

When it comes to getting a man to fall in love with you, it is not hard at all to integrate these secrets into your communication system and into your relationship.

Prepare and plan for your well-placed cues and flirts. You might even use a journal to come up with some creative ideas just as I have outlined it in my instructional video course that you might want to watch here:

Knowing about these secrets and what you need to do in order to tap into those emotional triggers is all you need to get him to fall in love with you and this is what you need to know in order to win his heart in the end.

Be the easygoing and natural girlfriend who does not sweat the small problems, and practice those secrets from above that will help you make him feel like the only man in your life. When he is confident about you and that you will return his feelings and affections by making him feel special with the little things that you do, he will not be able to help but fall head-over-heels in love with you. It is up to you how far you want this to happen and how much you want him commit to you. Just make sure that you always do it in an inspiring and empowering way so that no one gets hurt. You have lots of power over him in your hands so use it your benefit, but do not abuse it.

CHAPTER FOURTEEN

How Men Get Out Of The Friend Zone – Love Language 4

You thought that phobic commitment-phobe will never commit right?

False because there are secrets to unlocking even the most phobic commitment-phobe. Knowing these secrets can help you help him take that relationship to that next level that you both know you want.

Here is how you could recognize a man's behavior when he is trying to escape the friend
zone and is trying to get into the commitment zone. If he shows any of these signs, it means that he is really trying to get out of the friend zone and take the relationship with you to a new level.

The Secrets (Love Language 4)

1. If he tries to ask you if you ever thought of changing your status of your relationship, it is a sign that he is trying to tell you something. Go for it because he only suggests it if he is absolutely sure about what he is getting himself into otherwise he would not even bother.

2. Stop acting more interested than you really need to be.
This is referred to by scientists as the "Least Interested Principle". It has also been published by author Waller and author Hill in 1951. The principle goes like the following. If you are giving more value to one person than the other one is giving back to you, this relationship is already an unhealthy and a not balanced one because one person has the advantage over the other and can take control of things. Getting into an unhealthy relationship like this is never a good thing to begin with.

To regain power make sure and try this. It is called the least interested principle and it helps you with regaining power. Being less interested and less available and less accessible to him will enhance your value. He will understand how much he really does depend on you in the end.

3. Use the principle of scarcity and limit your time you spend with him. It is the simple concept of demand and supply really which works for time spent together, too. It is a psychological fact that men really want and desire what is put right in front of their eyes not as much and as intensive as men want something that is not in their immediate reach or that is not available to them instantly.

Cialdini, the well-known author of the title "Influence: Science and Practice," suggested in his book that the easiest way to manipulate and influence people was by utilizing a principle that is called "scarcity." The principle scarcity is the opposite of the law of abundance, but sometimes if you do not use the principle of scarcity abusively it might be effective.

It is exactly the same concept your mom used when she took away your favorite toys when you were not behaving proper. You wanted that toy or the TV even more once it was not reachable for you, even though you were not even planning on playing with it at that time, but the pure lack of it made you even more mad. It is the lack of power that drives us humans bad. Lesson learned here: make yourself scarce and you will become more valuable.

4. Create some competitive scenario and add lots of interest. It is important to make yourself scarce. When you become scarce and busy with others, your man will become more eager for your time and attention. Stack it up and you will see an immediate effect.

You can also start to test this concept out by really using this concept called "Social Proof." Start posting cute pictures of yourself on your social media wall with other "friends" of yours to see if your man says or does anything about it.

5. Ask your man for a couple of favors. Get him to invest time and energy in your person. A smart way to gauge if he wants to come out of the Friend Zone and into the Romantic Zone is to test if he is willing to invest in you.

This comes from science and it is called the Ben Franklin Effect. This research took place in 1969 and published in the issue of the Human Relations Journal. The Ben Franklin Effect does revolve around getting others to invest more of their time in your person.

By investing more time and energy in you, your person becomes automatically more meaningful to the other person. It is just like when you have to invest a little bit of money for a course instead of getting it for free. You are invested in it and you are determined to make it work. If you are obliged to invest in it, you will do everything to make that course work for you and especially if you do not have lots of money to begin with. This is the reason why savvy internet marketers offer you courses for $1 or they ask just for shipping and handling because they know that if you invest just a little bit, you will commit to their course and you will most likely succeed in the course. It is a win-win for everybody.

Men are attracted to women who mean something to them. Test his willingness to leave the Friend Zone by asking him a little favor or by finding a way to invest in your person. He may not jump into a romantic relationship with you overnight, but now he has an investment in you and will be more willing in the future to make it work. Researchers suggest that even asking him for something as simple as grabbing something for you from the kitchen will work just fine. You can always stack it up later. Start with little things and from there go to the bigger stuff.

As suggested in my video course, you might find it handy to use a journal to write down these things and how they affect your bottom line. If they work do more and if not adjust and do a little bit less and do it all in a natural and non-weird/obnoxious way!

The Bottom Line:

The bottom line is this. Whether he is your friend or a whether he is just a stranger, it is important to appeal to his emotional side. Using this strategy will most likely work in your favor when you are trying to solve the problem of how to get out of the friend zone. But it is also important to note the following. Make yourself not too available and present in his life. Make it not too easy for him to get to you. Make it not so easy for him to be friends with.

Making things too comfortable and too easy for him will work against you. Based on a situation like this he has no real interest, motivation or desire to leave the friend zone because he is comfortable just the way things are.

Use the scarcity principle that you learned above and the least interested principle, and sooner than later, you might find yourself surprised. You will discover that he is the one that makes the first step to reevaluate and renegotiate the terms of your newly discovered romantic relationship experience. If he does do not try

to be too anxious and too controlling about what has to go in there and what not. Make it a creative process and let the time spent with him and the experience of your new relationship manifest the how and the rules and the terms.

Think about it in terms of the law of abundance and the law of attraction where you have to let go of old rules and how to do stuff and rather focus on doing stuff with passion and with intention. Once you are capable of doing this and not just thinking about it and obsessing over it, you will not need to include some stupid rules that you wanted to include before. You know now that you can do without them and that they are not relevant to the development of your relationship anymore.

This self help and spirituality stuff is the stuff you should naturally build into your system and this is what I am talking about when I talk about integrating it little by little. I refer to this process in my video course and now you should be clear on how this process works. It should not be a threatening or intimidating process because it might be threatening to you at first and when you hear about these new concepts like the law of attraction etc. for the very first time.

Just be open to integrate some new and positive success factors that I will gradually be introducing to you and stack them on top of what already works for you and you can't help but be successful at what you are doing.

Right now you are in the process of attracting and transforming love from one state to another and just know that you keep attracting what you want to attract because it is like a reflection. If you are positive about it then it comes back to you like a reflection.

I need you with an open mind because I will introduce little by little more and more success principles that might come from another school of thought like from the spirituality area. Just be open about it and pick little things at first and try it and note down your successes. You will want to hear more about it and scale up once you see the results.

Chapter Fivteen

How Men Love And Commit – Love Language Five

Decoding a guy's action can cause bad headaches for most of us women. It is because men are really not that articulate about things as women would express her feelings in words.

Have you ever heard a man say that women are like dictionaries? It is true men rely on action and do not need words to express what they do and women rely on an array of words with lots of adjectives in order to describe the character and the beauty of things.

This wordiness is driving men nuts because they are problem solvers. That is why most verbal fights between men and women start. A man wants to solve the problem while the woman just wants to talk about any possible aspect of it.

If you keep on asking, "How do men show love then?" There are some pretty obvious affection detection hints that a man just can not hide from you.

Lots of studies have been done on this topic and all of them show that men do not rely on words to express their feelings. Men are action oriented while women are oriented in feelings and emotions. Feelings for men call or trigger their action. That is why, when you want to talk about your feelings with your sweetheart, he reacts weird as if he had to solve a problem via taking action. He interprets feelings that are a problem that he needs to be solving in a physical way. It never occurs to him that using words and a dialog is an opportunity to build emotional closeness that women are seeking.

So how do men show love then?

Let me answer this with a situation so you understand the difference via an explicit example. When a woman asked a man I knew whether he loved her, wanting him to say the words, he just responded without giving it any further though, "Have you not been paying attention to what I have been doing?"

It is more often a matter of how men interpret the world around them and what is meaningful to them and the communication style of how they express their world and their actions rather than a men's commitment issue.

The Secrets (Love Language 5)

1. He lends his most valuable & beloved things to You

Among us, humans, control of our property is a part of ourselves and our society.

Why do you think so many men carry weapons? It is not to kill people, but to protect his stuff in most cases.

If he lends you his iPad or his favorite shirt, he has entrusted an important part of himself to you.
He has expressed vulnerability, knowing full well that you could even lose his possession, and that would hurt him, but nevertheless he trusts you and he is willing to give it to you.

2. Having taken his picture with You

A typical man will have a twisted perception with a camera because it can spy on him. He does not trust it right away. At one point, he may be rushing to pose, but when it comes to being open to a great photo opportunity with his woman, he can be a bit nervous and intimidated. Why is that? It is because a man usually wants to project being single not in a couple even though he is involved.
He is worried by the thought of when he wraps his arm around you for a cam shot, he might be sending a signal to everyone that he is off the market which is a very scary thought for a man.

3. He Wants To Keep You Safe

Since the earliest days of our human species, men have always protected their women. The prince who safeguards the enslaved girl is not just a woman's fantasy. It is real. Don't be surprised when he gives you a gift that is full of man stuff like pepper spray, tear gas, personal alarms or stun gun. This only means that he wanted to keep you protected and safe when he might not be there to do it. His own security reflexes are so important to him so that he might end up giving you stuff like self-defense tools and security gadgets and other survival stuff that he learned about from reading books like how to live off the grid and the survival prepper bible. In his mind, he has no idea that these prepper gifts are not more romantic than the usual chocolates and flowers that you desire and expect.

4. When Eating, He Sits Beside You Not Opposite

Have you noticed that women together always sit facing each other, looking into each other's eyes and faces, sharing their feelings and having a bubbly talk while he prefers to sit side by side? He wants to be able to touch you and share food with you.

Did you know that early in dating, a man will sit across from you, but little by little he will change his habit and when he becomes comfortable with you, he will want to sit beside you.

To us women that might sound weird, but make a mental note about it and see for yourself.

Sharing a meal has always been a fundamental human ritual, expressing and building community and society. Sharing meals goes back to the beginnings of our human species.
where males had the roles of hunters and were bringing back their treasures to share with their women, children, and the whole community. Be aware that when he changes his position that he is symbolically providing and caring for you.

5. Love is hard to hide

When a man has intense feelings for you, he's more likely to show you with actions than to tell you with words.

Remember we talked about this earlier!

You on the other hand, want to know if he is romantic. If he compliments you. If he makes you feel special?
If he does, these are all good signs that your relationship is on a healthy track. Like I told you before in order to get his love you should do things like emphasizing or acknowledging or complimenting him on his efforts.

6. When a man loves You

He will seek to meet your needs as well as his own in a balanced way. If he does this then this is a good sign for you. When he is asking for your opinion on things or when he tries to make sure that you are comfortable then he really is into you. Look at how he responds when you are sick or when you are in a bad mood? If he brings you flowers or a gift or if he calls to check on you, that is his way of letting you know that you are his woman and that he loves and accepts you.

7. When man loves You

He wants to know everything about you, about your dreams, about your goals, about your world view and since he is the action taker he will also try to help you achieve success. Men are problem solvers and men will be supportive.
They hate to see you sitting there unhappy or disappointed or frustrated so they always look for ways how to relieve your stress and help you address the issues at hand. They either tell you Let Me Help You or they give you the How to of the problem outlined in action steps.

8. When a man loves you, he will respond to Your emotional needs

Does your man do his very best to make you feel protected and secure? Does he comfort you when you are mad, sad, unhappy, or upset about your work or life in general? Or does he run for the hills?
If he stays at your side during times of trouble and when you are not emotionally balanced, that is a very good sign that he really loves you and wants to do everything to make you feel better.

9. When a man loves you, he'll make a commitment to You

He may not be ready for marriage yet, but he also is not out exploring his options with other women because he is committed to you.

Love can be more than complex and complicated at the same times. If you are in doubt about where your love and your relationship is at, take your time and discover if you recognize some, a few or all of these secret signs that tell you that he loves you. Keep in mind though that you never seem to see them all at once. Yes it might happen to a few of us, but mostly in fairy tales so be real about your expectation and your goals because it is never perfect and that is because love typically happens in stages and you are evolving and developing and transforming your love from one state to another one.

The bottom line with men though and you can count on that proof is if he loves you, see what he does.

Chapter Sixteen

How Men Love Forever & Never Lose Interest – Love Language 6

How does a man love you forever you might ask. If you do respect some basic rules, you can achieve a level of love where he will be committed forever. Some call it eternal love, others call it dream marriage, while still others refer to it as the love of their life. No matter how people call this stage, it is more important to understand the underlying principles than giving it a perfect name.

Once you have an idea of what to do, put it into practice and watch your relationship change for the better.

The Secrets - Love Language 6

Acceptance

Don't you know it when too often you get together with a man who strikes your fancy, thinking that he is lovely and nice and has good manners if only for... and then think that you can "fix the thing" and you can change the man so that he is "perfect.

Wrong approach girl! Instead, learn to accept and respect him. Get over it and accept the man for who he is and what he stands for. If he really is not the guy for you, then have an honest conversation with him instead of settling for second best.

If it is about the small stuff you must learn to accept and live with it. If you accept him and his values you will tap into the win win situation because acceptance is just one secret you absolutely must know about in order to grow your relationship into one that is forever lasting.

Inter-dependence

As much as you like being together, it is critical for you and him to have time to yourselves. You want to cultivating hobbies, interests, career, job, business and you want to maintain other social engagements and other friendships without him. You can be together with him and still have time for other things in life, too.

In the end was it not the reason to come together and spend time with your man because you choose to be with him, not because you need to or because you are dependent on him?

Ask yourself these types of questions and you will be on the right track of everlasting love.

Communication

It is a, accepted concept that God created us with 2 ears but only one mouth (listen more than speak?) and that we need to be careful in our choice of words.

As we have been seeing through the years we know that there is a lot of power in words. Words can start wars and they can not be easily retracted. You feel bad after having insulted someone and you run the scenario countless times through your head because the words you used reflect upon you.

Be careful and loving in the things you say and how you say them and also be aware of your body language and your tone because this all makes up communication and how he interprets your spoken words and your unspoken signals.

Always use positive, inspirational and engaging content to spice up and make your conversation interesting. Give each other opportunities to listen, understand, comprehend, interpret as well as comment and share doubts, thought, feelings, dreams, goals, visions and perspectives.

If you have issues with your communication, deal with them in a loving and caring and explaining way without blaming or even worth without insulting each other.

Communication is a tool and should always be used in a positive and empowering way so make a habit out of it and use it to empower both of you.

Tolerance

Just because your guy loves you, does not really mean that each of you will fall in total love and passion with each other's siblings. As long as you can accept the other family and can be polite and respectful when you meet them, you are good to go. As you can see tolerance is a very powerful quality that qualifies you to be that woman that he never loses interest about.

Transparency

Be honest and open with your man and do not resort to playing mind games because that might backfire on you. If you try to manipulate your relationship with your man in a negative and in a forcing way in order to get what you want, you risk losing him.
He will not know who you are and if he can trust you. He will catch you and more than likely lose respect in you and leave you. Men are not really into playing crazy mind games based on drama. Watch out for men who are into this because you can not base your love on such principles and negativity. If you are practicing an open mind and if you are transparent about your actions, you will absolutely make him want to be with you in the long run.

Make sure to include all these 5 secrets in your day to day ritual and learn how to become better at each of these principles and skills. There are great courses out there online that will show you how to fine-tune these skills and master them with whatever you are trying to achieve.

These are the basic stepping stone secrets that you need to be aware of and cultivate if you are serious about catapulting your relationship into the stratosphere.

These 5 secrets are the chore principles that you absolutely need to know about and from where you can go into whatever you want to achieve and whenever you want to achieve it. Master these 5 secrets and he will give the world to you. You can demand everything you want from him and he will make sure to give it to you if you do your homework and start integrating these 5 chores into your system and if you get better at them. You just need to apply them naturally and pepper them into your relationship as you go about your day. Once you really master them you will see his reaction to you and that is when you know that your relationship is real and there to last forever.

Remember not to obnoxiously and abusively use these principles and the skills that you have been developing from them because this system will only work if you use your tools in a natural and subtle way. Never abuse or obsess over your knowledge or take too much power from these secrets. Abusing secrets and power as well as forcing others into something is never the proper solution.

This whole love language system only works if you apply it little by little and as natural as you can. You will see the big AHA moment as you use your writing journal and as you progress. It is little things that you will be changing and little things that will be working and that you will be doing that you stack together and that will accumulate over time and then you will see your love manifest in a way that is not dependent on time and that some folks call **Eternal Love.**

Chapter Seventeen

One More Thing

That's it folks...

Remember not to obnoxiously and abusively use these principles and the skills that you have been developing from them because this system will only work if you use your tools in a natural and subtle way. Never abuse or obsess over your knowledge or take too much power from these secrets. Abusing secrets and power as well as forcing others into something is never an empowering solution.

This whole love language system only works if you apply it little by little and as natural as you can. You will see the big AHA moment as you use your writing journal and as you progress. It is little things that you will be changing and little things that will be working and that you will be doing that you stack together and that will accumulate over time and then you will see your love manifest in a way that is not dependent on time and that some folks call **eternal love.**

ONE MORE THING

And just some last important things that you absolutely must work on if you have an issue with it because if you don't deal with it right now, transforming your love into eternal love will not work for you.

I am here to help and empower you get what you desire and want and I can only help you if you make a small effort every day. You will see later how important those little steps are because you have to reach the zone from where even more powerful things are possible.

You have to reach the zone of abundance.

You will reach it soon and I will teach you much more about it if you work on this attraction system day by day and from your daily achievements you will get into the abundance zone from where you will be able to manifest everything and as much as you want. There are no limits!

All you have to be concerned yourself with for now is getting better and the basic module 1 and the secrets module 2. From there you can scale it up into the abundance mindset and I will be teaching you more and more about how to do put everything together. The greatest power is coming from there. The languages of abundant love will make you ask questions like:

How much love do I want to receive?

How many opportunities do I want to pursue?

It is not a matter of can I get love at all anymore. It is going to be a matter of how much where you decide how much is enough for you.

When you started with this book your question might have been is love possible for me at at all.

The next question would be how much do I actually want because I can have unlimited love and an abundance of love.

I hope by now you can already see the transformation that is taking shape here.

By going through this system you can answer your initial question and the self-doubting question with a resounding YES by now.

You have gone through the whole system that empowers you to **get what you want** via **understanding what he really wants.**

Not only has your answer been answered, but by applying the system you are now able to attract, make him fall in love, make him leave the friend zone and commit, and make him love you forever.

Now you have the tools, the principles, the secrets and the skills that you need to apply so I encourage you to get started from here by keeping a journal and track your progress daily. It does not matter what stage you are, just go from where you are and apply what is most relevant to your goal and situation.

Do little things every day and see how your relationship changes over time. Track your progress and see how these little things will accumulate over time.

Give yourself at least 4 months to go over the course by applying it and at least one week per love language. Remember this is not a sprint it is a marathon and a lifelong learning process.

After having applied little new things on a daily basis and changing old non-working habits into new ones, you will see results and these results will help you stay on track, stay motivated and inspired and never forget to reward yourself for achieving little goals.

Once you are really good at getting what you want from him, you should ask yourself how can I scale this up and that is the time when your questions will become more powerful and your desire to experience more things will increase and your leverage factor will become more powerful because by now you will be able to tap into so many powerful secrets.

But you can tap into even more power. Keep your desire, experience and leverage factor that you tapped into this course on power, but buckle up and get ready for more.

Stack more powerful tools on top of everything you already have in place by now.

So, where to go from the point of all goes well and this system works well for you and you have catapulted your relationship in the right direction and you are now enabled to get everything you want from him.

Where to go from here?

I suggest you watch my free video course where I talk to you about even more powerful stuff (law of attraction and love, abundant love, and lots more) and that is where your journey continues...

From there you will be able to tap into the really powerful stuff. From there you will be capable to command and control an even greater power. You can actually quantify how much you want of all and get it all! Your man will hand it to you without any resistance and you can control how much of it you want!

This is how powerful this next level information is. You are qualified by now to take this powerful course because you have already changed your mindset and actions and you do not have any doubts anymore. All the negativity surrounding this topic and all myths have been busted and turned into a deep and rich attraction system for you powered by the 6 love languages.

Congratulations on having completed the course and I hope you will get lots of opportunities for your love life and your relationship out of it.

If you do it right you can command everything in a positive and empowering way from now on and you will get it from him because you are applying the correct code and the correct psychological tricks that will get you what you want without ignoring his desires.

It will work for you because you are doing it in the proper balanced and positive way like I am teaching it.

This is the only way to go because using too much power and trying to manipulate him will backfire on you and all your time and energy is going to be wasted so make sure to lay-out your goals and you plan as discussed in module 1 first and then get to the specifics and the how to type of information in part 2.

Finally live your experience in combination with a writing journal and finetune the process.

From there you can go anywhere you like next because now you are ready for the next more powerful attraction information that I would love to share with you if you like what you have been learning so far. You can connect with me by visiting the Connect chapter in this book and connect from there.

To all your attraction success,

Emmie Martins

Chapter Eighteen

Bonus 1: 19 Rules For Winning His Heart Forever

Decoding a guy's action can cause bad headaches for most of us women. It is because men are really not that articulate about things as women would express her feelings in words. So here are the 19 most important clues to decode him.

You being as cute as You can be at his side

He is proud to have you in his arms. He will want to show this to his friends. He just loves to show you off even more though if you look and act in such a manner that you will be drawing admiring looks from the people around. The fact that you belong to him (ego thing) and are able to turn heads towards his couple that he is so proud of is enough reason for him to stay on your side. In his mind you belong to him.

Understand him and be and patient

A woman can only have success in keeping and sustaining her relationship with a man when she is taking the time to listen and understand her man from her heart. Alway be patient with him and loving while you are dealing with your man and make certain that you do not make rash conclusions and judgments and wrong assumptions about how he is acting. This understanding and loving attitude will make your man admire you even more.
He is considering himself very lucky to have you when you are acting like described.

Loving him with all Your heart

There is nothing in the whole world that can take the place of a true love. He will instinctively know if you are true about your feelings and if your love is true. He will know if you care for him. Unless you are honest with your man and with your own proper feelings you will never be able to reach complete satisfaction in him satisfy him. It is when you really love him that you will find it easier to go the one extra mile that it takes to make a difference. If you do show him that extra care he will feel special.

Stand by him and let him know

Why do men get disappointed with a woman in the first place? Well, he feels being let down by her because when the going gets tough he is finding himself all alone. Do not let a situation like this happen to you. If you really want to win his heart make sure to prove to him that you are the type of woman who is different because you will be able to stand by your man and no matter how tough it is.

Sexual fantasy? Dare to be his

The hard hitting truth is this if a man is sexually satisfied he is not going to feel a sexual need that he has to fill with another woman! Make sure the physical attraction and chemistry between you and him is as exciting and strong as ever! It is important to look sexually as appealing as in the beginning. Make sure he will find it hard to resist you or take off his mind of your eyes!

Earn his respect & trust

If he knows that he can trust you, he loves you even deeper. Not only will he know deep in his heart that you will never do the cheating part on him, but your man will be more relaxed and enjoy your companionship even more knowing that he might risk losing you to another man.
The trust factor is the basis of any functioning relationship and the trust is what keeps a couple together.

Never let down Your man in any way, shape, or form

If you disappoint him and a let him down constantly there is no way he is going to put up with him. If on the other hand you are there for him and if you make sure that you are honest and trustworthy, you can get everything from him you ever want. You must find a way to satisfy him on all levels and that is intellectually as well as physically.

Super confident women are amazing

Most of us lack self-confidence. We would like to change so many things that we hate about ourselves. Do not let him become aware of your lack of confidence. You want him super interested in you and you want him to see you as someone who is super happy with yourself. You do not want to point out your flaws. Embracing your real you is always better than beating yourself up.

Always be honest to him

Do not try to impress him by false claims or exaggeration. It is not going to work in the end. He will see right through your games. Instead, present yourself natural and show your passion. Act real and exactly the way you are. Being genuine, helpful, honest and real is the only way to go.
He will actually find it incredibly refreshing to be with someone who is not artificial and not congruent in action and word.

Always be fun to be around

No man wants to ever spend his valuable time around a drama queen. There is just no fun to be had in such a pitiful environment. Do leave worries at home and let your man see your smile and laugh instead. The more fun you are having with him, the more time he is going to want to spend with his girl.

Always be kind

The power of kindness is limitless and abundant. Your man wants his woman with a quality of kindness. He craves your kindness. Me love being around a woman who treats people nicely. If you are offering a helping hand and he sees that he will let you in his gear big time.

Do not show You are jealousy

The world will always be full of other attractive ladies and you know it. He is going to look sometimes and that is just the way the brain of a man functions. You have to accept it. Do not let jealousy control your relationship. He will see it as a sign of lack of confidence and
self-esteem. Such a quality looks completely unattractive to a man. Work on your jealousy issues and never let him notice.

Be an adventurous girl

Men love the outdoors and adventure. A woman who sits at home all the time is not attractive to a man.

Step outside your own comfort zone and go on some adventures with him. Spontaneity is what a man looks for. He loves to be surprised so make sure to come up with some exciting weekend plans. Make sure to do this from time to time so he can enjoy spending some time on an adventure with you.

Be a supportive girl

A man longs to be with a woman who needs him. You might be very self-sufficient, but still let him be there for you sometimes and ask for a little help here and there. Regularly, ask him to help you with some smaller tasks and do the same for him because he needs support from you, too. The key is to find a balance of give and take like with anything in life. He is going to want to give as much of his person to you as he possibly can and you should do the same for him.

Never rush it

Guys do not like to be pushed into the relationship stuff. They even freak out about it. Take it slow in the beginning. It is not a race, but it is a process that takes on forever because it is a life-long learning experience. Do not hurry him or he will run for the hills. Let him lead you because this is his role. He is only going to be ready for the next step if you let him do this.

Never use sex to control, manipulate, or tie him to You

Sex is better when you are both connected. It is even better when you are connected on an emotional level. I can tell you right now the physical aspect of the relationship is going to fade away, but the emotional level will make up for this. If you do not put any emotional effort into your sexual relationship, you will be left with a huge emotional pitiful void. Only engage in a sexual relationship if you are mentally ready for it and never base it on pure sex alone.

Be a self confidence girl

Men find independent women attractive. A man loves it when his girl is confident. It tells him that you are not going to depending on him. Before you egage in a serious relationship, you must absolutely be sure about what you want to do with your life. The guy will respect you more if you know what you want out of life.

Always lend your ear

The basis for a relationship has to be a two way road. It can never be about one person only. You always have to be patient and listen to what your partner has to say. Make him comfortable by talking to him and understanding his point of view. If you are there for him, he will know that he matter to you and such a confirmation is important for the health of your relationship.

Always support him

A man will judge you and that is just a matter of life and human mind. Be conscient about the fact that he will judge you character, too. You absolutely must support him when he needs it the most or when he is at a fragile time in his life. Make it absolutely clear to him that you will stick with him. When he is feeling down due to work, stress or people, give him a nice break and hug him. What else can you do? You could offer your man a nice massage with his favorite music turned on. There is a great saying that expresses what the support factor is all about "Behind every successful man is a woman".
You have the power to support him and you can take many ways to do it. Just get creative about it and you will find and abundant amount of ideas.

Always listen to him

When you listen to your man, he develops more affection and trust for you. Unfortunately, most females are talkers only and not listeners. They assume and do not really listen. They do not get the facts straight. They prefer to talk about their oh so important problems and their own life and forget that a relationship is about give and take. They do not really care about the man's problems. If you are like that woman who does that, please stop it today. Listening to your man is one skill that will help enrich your relationship. Allow your man to share his feelings with you and you will grow in directions that you never thought possible. Get to know him and get to appreciate him by listening to his problems and his point of view.

Never Ever be the clingy girl

Never be the clingy girl. If you act clingy with a guy, he will feel total desperation. If you are obnoxiously clingy he will leave you quicker as you can think about it. If you keep messaging him all day and be really weird about it or if you want to talk to him all day every day long, it will send a clear message to him telling him that you are a needy and desperate girl. It will tell him that you are desperate for his attention and he will take his consequences. A needy girl is getting in his way and taking up all his energy so he feels blocked and not functioning well.
I told you before men need to act in order to provide so do not get into his way with your lack of self confidence and find a passion of your own that he can be proud of. He will try to avoid you as much as possible if you let him not do his thing.

Make sure to look good when it is important

Your man will love you more and more and more if you try better and better to do your best to look good for him because it will reflect upon him. Make sure that you dress in a choice of clothing that is in very good condition, clean and that does not reveal too much of your body. Be attractive, but not too revealing. He will appreciate your good taste. Also make sure to ask him for his point of view on your clothing choice and make an effort to wear the clothes that he likes seeing on you. If necessary, get advice from a pro or look for a complete makeover.

If you respect all these 19 rules above, you can't help but transform yourself which is the best thing that can happen to you because you need to get to the next level in order to keep a relationship healthy.

Take responsibility in your personal development and all the other skills that are necessary in order to develop like talked about in module 1 and 2 of this course. You are the only one who can put power into this and only if you take yourself to the next level can you bring your relationship to the next level.

If you want to learn more about next level stuff, make sure to start with my free video course that walks you through the next level information.

Chapter Ninteen

Bonus 2: Conversation Starters For Every Occasion

Conversation Starters For All Stages Of Your Relationship To Build Deep & Rich & True Love That Lasts Forever...

70 Secret Romantic Phrases & Conversation Starters that you can apply to any relationship stage you might find yourself in.

Go through them and find your own application and put it in your toolbox and your daily routine.

Don't abuse and influence your man too much with these phrases because if you exaggerate and abuse, you will not sound natural anymore and your partner will see right through it.

You have a powerful tool in your hands so make sure to use it with care and in a way that does not make you look foolish.

I remind you about the fact that if you want your man to love you forever, communication is of utmost importance. To make him addicted to you, you must practice communicative skills and you must attract him and make him interested in your message.

The words and phrases below used effectively will win his heart. Be creative about it and make your own versions by stacking and matching phrases together to make the message even more powerful...

Adapt and fit to your relationship stage and chose what suits your personality and communication style best.

70 Secret Phrases That Will Win His Heart Forever:

1. All I care about is that I can not live without you anymore.
2. I just want to be with you forever.
3. All the diamonds and all the gold and all the bitcoins are not enough to buy the love
    that I carry for you in my heart.

4. I believe in God because he created you just for me.
5. I am not only addicted to your love, I am obsessed!
6. OMG, I am so crazy about you and can't stop thinking about you.
7. I can not live without you because you are like my oxygen.
8. All I really care about is being with you for now and forever.
9. I can not stop thinking about you my love.
10. I did not mean to hurt your feelings my sweetheart.
11. I do not ever want to wake up from this wonderful dream that I am living with you.
12. I only feel safe when I can be with you.
13. Each time I get lost in ecstasy when you make love to me like a God
14. You have shown me what true love really is. I have finally discovered it!
15. I not only enjoy talking with you, but I love talking to you.
16. I am thrilled by the way you are making love to me.
17. I miss your hugs and kisses and words when life gets between us.
18. I thank heaven for that day you were brought into my life because you enlighten it.
19. I want to spend the rest of my life with you - that is forever!
20. I would give my most precious possessions just to be with you.
21. You already have my heart, and I will give you my body, and my soul.
22. I will join you to the ends of the world
23. I would never trade your love for a million dollars.
24. I will travel a thousand miles to be able to touch you and be with you.
25. I wish I had met you sooner.
26. I am going crazy for you.
27. If I could I would make love to you a thousand times, but I am just a woman.
28. If I had to live this wonderful life over and over again like a reincarnation, I would choose to live it only with you.
29. If loving you is really considered a sin, then let me be guilty as hell.
30. If our love is blind and dark like the night, then I never want it to see the light of day ever again.
31. Life without having you on my side would be like going to sleep without sweet dreams - awful!
32. Loving you feels like sweeter than heaven.
33. Loving you has made my life so much sweeter.
34. Loving you has made my life so full of joy and so full of happiness and joy.
35. My heart cries when we have to drift apart.

36. You are my joy, you are my love, you are my heart, and you are my life.
37. No man has ever loved me the way you love me when you do!
38. Nothing in this world has the power to stop me from loving you.
39. Oh sweetie pie, you are the best love that ever happened to me.
40. Do you know that your tender kisses and soft touches are more precious than gold could ever be?
41. Talking to you my love is like sipping the most delicious champagne. A joyful time that I want to last forever.
42. The times we are spending together are to me like the most precious stones. Money can never buy a love like this!
43. Time stops for me when you hold me, and when you touch me, and when you kiss me
44. When I am with you my love, my troubles always seem to fade away.
45. When I look at you each time, I can see a man that I find irresistibly handsome and kind.
46. Words are not enough to express my love for you.
47. You are my prince! Come and save me!
48. You are my soul mate who brings sense into my life.
49. You are the most important man in my life.
50. You are the rhythm, the sound, and the true meaning of the music that makes my heart beat.
51. You are the only man I ever want to spend my life with.
52. Without you I would only be half because You are the other half that makes me whole.
53. You are the perfect man for me because you make me whole.
54. You are the sweetest man I know and the kindest man I know and that's why I belong to   you.
55. You bring nothing but love, peace, joy, happiness, and insight to my soul.
56. You bring so much happiness and enlightenment to my life and I feel so happy.
57. You love me gently, you love me truly, you love me tender, you love me like a man should do.
58. You make me feel like a woman because you love me the way you do.
59. You make me feel so good, you make me feel so happy. I want to kiss you from your head to your hip and from there to the tips of your toes.
60. You make me want you more each day. You make me want you even more tomorrow.

61. You treat me like a princess with your tender heart and I your love makes me feel worth like a million.
62. You're the kindest man I know. You're the most caring man I have ever spoken to. You're the most insightful man I can ever trust. You're my true passion and love.
63. Your caring words touch the deepest part of me. Tomorrow you will conquer my soul!
64. Your tender hugs and your sweet kisses are melting my heart. My heart seems to melt away like the sweetest fondant chocolate treat.
65. Your sweet kiss is tasting better than the most superior Swiss chocolate dream enjoyed on a cold winter moonlight night.
66. Your kisses feel so good to my soul. Your kisses feel like a fountain of tingles all over my body.
67. Your love is like a giant rock that stands out bold and strong. Our love is too powerful to ever break it.
68. Your love is so true and pure I can not get away from you even if I wanted to.
69. Your love fills my body with warm sunshine. Your love fills my heart with the glow of a candlelight. Your love gives me the reason to live. Your love is like a midsummer night's dream.
70. Your whispers of loving words in a moonlight night are soothing me like honey; Your sweet words put me in the mood of dreaming about you.
71. Your smile is so comforting. Your smile is so revealing. Your smile even makes my worries and tears fade away.
72. Your gentle touches send out chills and my whole body from head down to my spine is awake feeling that sensational mood of loving you.

Add your own and stack and match by using a personal journal where you can write down your progress and become a better communicator. You can not only track your communication skills via such a journal, but you can make powerful lists of phrases just like the ones above. You can also make lists of your own phrases that you find work best for you!

Check out the Other Books chapter to check out some journals that might strike your fancy...

Acknowledgments

We support copyright of all intellectual property. Copyright protection continues to spark the seed of creativity in content producers, ensures that everyone has their voice heard through the power of words and the captivity of a story. Uniqueness of culture and content has been passed down through generations of storytelling and is the DNA of every intelligent species on our planet.

This publication is intended to provide helpful and informative material. It is not intended to diagnose, treat, cure, or prevent any health problem or condition, nor is intended to replace the advice of a physician. No action should be taken solely on the contents of this book. Always consult your physician or qualified health-care professional on any matters regarding your health and before adopting any suggestions in this book or drawing inferences from it.

www.ingramcontent.com/pod-product-compliance
Lightning Source LLC
LaVergne TN
LVHW060336080526
838202LV00053B/4482